NEW ORLEANS
CLASSICS

TENOR SAXOPHONE
SOLO

MUSIC MINUS ONE

mmo
4221

SUGGESTIONS FOR USING THIS MMO EDITION

*W*E HAVE TRIED to create a product that will provide you an easy way to learn and perform these compositions with a full ensemble in the comfort of your own home. Because it involves a fixed accompaniment performance, there is an inherent lack of flexibility in tempo. The following MMO features and techniques will reduce these inflexibilities and help you maximize the effectiveness of the MMO practice and performance system:

We have observed generally accepted tempi, and always in the originally intended key, but some may wish to perform at a different tempo, or to slow down or speed up the accompaniment for practice purposes; or to alter the piece to a more comfortable key. We have included slow-tempo versions of the most up-tempo pieces on this album for practice and/or a slower interpretation. But for even more flexibility, you can purchase from MMO specialized CD players & recorders which allow variable speed while maintaining proper pitch, and vice versa. This is an indispensable tool for the serious musician and you may wish to look into purchasing this useful piece of equipment for full enjoyment of all your MMO editions.

We want to provide you with the most useful practice and performance accompaniments possible. If you have any suggestions for improving the MMO system, please feel free to contact us. You can reach us by e-mail at info@musicminusone.com.

mmo
4221

CONTENTS

Tenor Saxophone in B♭

Fidgety Feet

Original Dixieland Jass Band

TENOR SAXOPHONE IN B♭

Tin Roof Blues

New Orleans Rhythm Kings

CLARINET SOLO

TROMBONE SOLO

Tenor Saxophone in B♭

Royal Garden Blues

Clarence & Spencer Williams

Tenor Saxophone in Bb

Blue Orleans

Tim Laughlin

MMO 4221

Tenor Saxophone in B♭

Dumaine Street Breakdown

Tim Laughlin

Tenor Saxophone in B♭

Savoy Blues

Edward "Kid" Ory

Tenor Saxophone in Bb

March of the Uncle Bubbys

Tim Laughlin

Do You Know What It Means to Miss New Orleans?

Eddie DeLang
Louis Alter

Tenor Saxophone in Bb

Someday You'll Be Sorry

DIXIELAND BAND-ENSEMBLE

LOUIS ARMSTRONG

TENOR SAX SOLO

PIANO SOLO

CORNET SOLO

DIXIELAND BAND-ENSEMBLE

TENOR SAXOPHONE IN Bb

Quincy Street Stomp

SIDNEY BECHET

23

MMO 4221

MUSIC MINUS ONE
50 Executive Boulevard
Elmsford, New York 10523-1325
1.800.669.7464 (U.S.)/914.592.1188 (International)

www.musicminusone.com
e-mail: mmogroup@musicminusone.com